HEATHER

A poetic cwtch

BY JASNA USMAN

Illustrations and cover design by Jasna Usman

ISBN: 978-93-5701-188-4

jasnausman98@gmail.com

To the ones I call mine…

CONTENT

THE RISING

Her confessions
were as strong as the Northerly gale
even the finest fillets
got lured away

Dreams that kept me awake
were dying for me to be open

Your wildflowers came seeking
for the poet hiding -
miles beneath the Roman walls

The breeze assuaged her fears
and the truth beguiled the shores
'she was a living fairytale
in her own parallel world'

Mellowed was her gentle beige
as the desperate violets bloomed ecstasy

Kissed by fire
rarest one could find
spasms spoke louder
than the tension built
drawn to her charismatic smile
and yet vulnerable to the tint;
A Caribbean blue
hiding behind her faded tattoo

The silver platter in my ambry
showed me the noble steed
sleeping for a while
whose cwtch dazzled the hearts
across a thousand miles

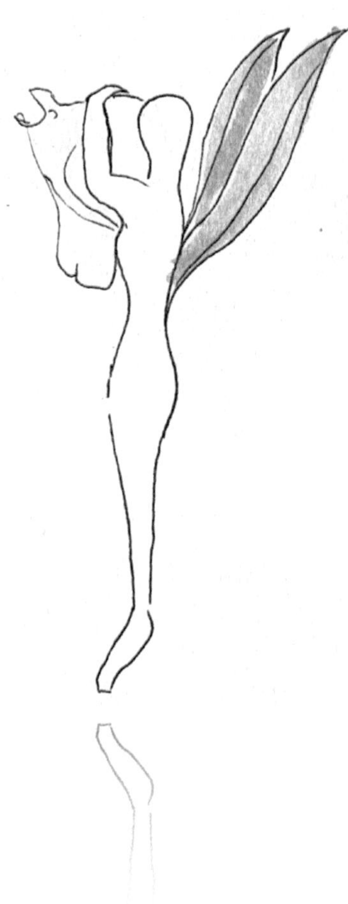

Sailing
past the levee
through the labyrinth
amongst the Northern stars

(found her)

Chasing you is my favourite adventure

- to self love

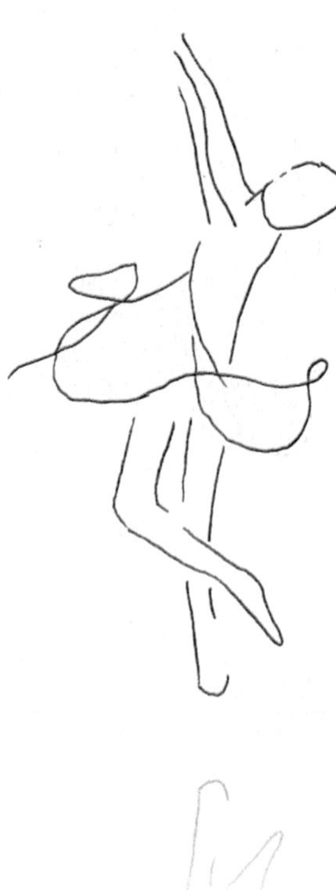

She dreamt of riding
past the dragons
a puzzled epilogue
thawed
the rime on her lashes;
‘unveiled the gazelle beneath’

Does your story start with
'Once upon a time?'

Symphony in the bulbil's ire
hovering in azure blue
whimpered to break open
your catacomb -
down the narrow dell

The resonating crunch
filled in the voids
as your sinews
rose from the ashes
forever anew

Fallen for you
and hereby leaving the trails
I'm sorry, but
you have to me go;
bid your byes for now
hoping to meet again
from the skies above

She sought solace in blue
whilst rewriting her story
stone cold -
a grieving canoe
floating on her wilted blooms

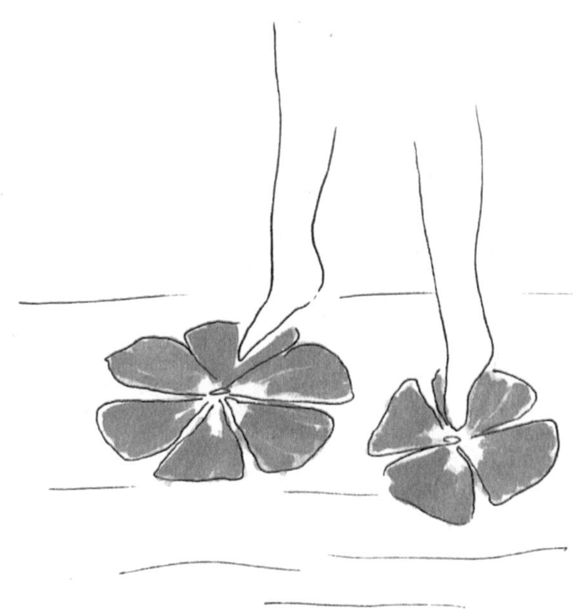

Stop
being the menace to my wings
let me fly
at least for a while

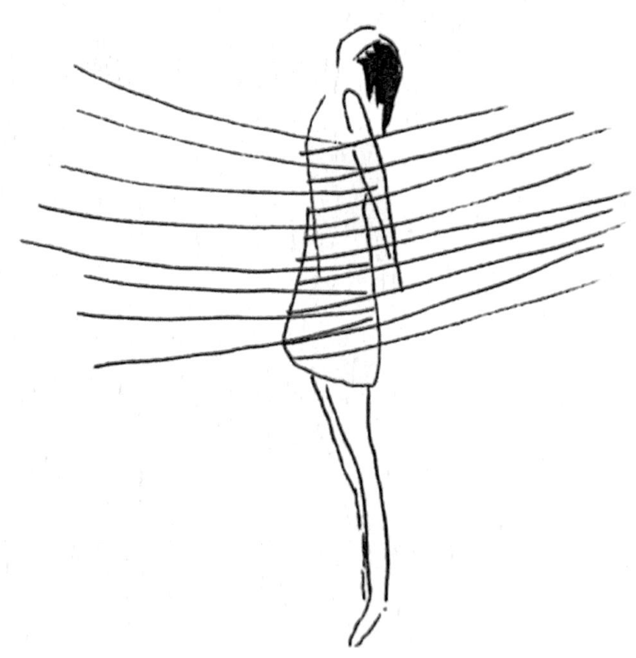

I travelled back
like half a decade
and in that delicate seizure
I saw the poet in me

And like a feather
I'll fly
maybe without gravity this time

(pale wishes)

THE SETTING

Sitting on the roof top
watching city lights
wearing dusk
and you by my side;
picture perfect

(the ones that I still hold onto)

I'm a blank canvas
desperate for the silver brushes
to soak me in the colours
I fell in love with

I miss being yours
I'll tell you another tale
or even paint you
an ocean
in rhyming dusky shades

(conversations)

Yet another dance we chose
strangling the vows
epic it seemed
brewing that one last kiss

Oh Monsieur!
your bemused touch
seasoned my parting thoughts
and my mirror image

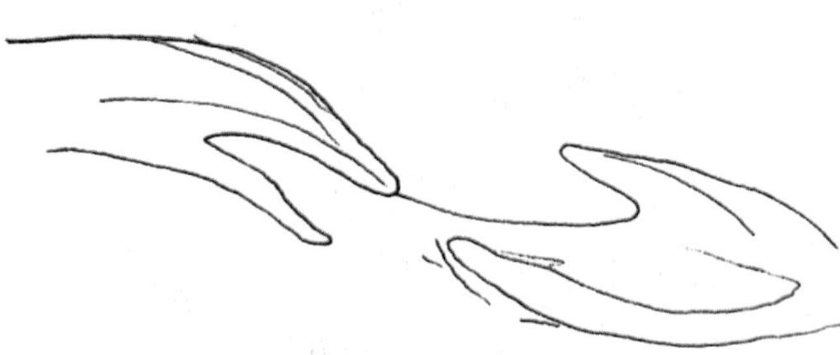

Am the art
speaking in silence
like a crescent mage
chanting spells after spells
'may we meet again'

From horizons afar,
where my land behold your sky
I'll whisper another one of my lies
'you and I'

(why do we always have to rhyme?)

A moment halfway blooming
vows and floating lanterns
and you walking down the aisle

(It's you, it has always been you)

The tint
the shade
the azure
my love, this eve
we were meant to be
the crimson in the setting sun

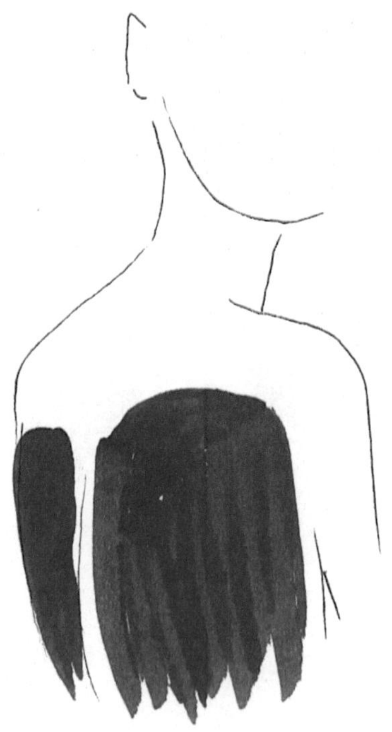

Phosphenes in eyes
lingering touch
magical heathers
blooming on my bruises

(Am healing in your kiss)

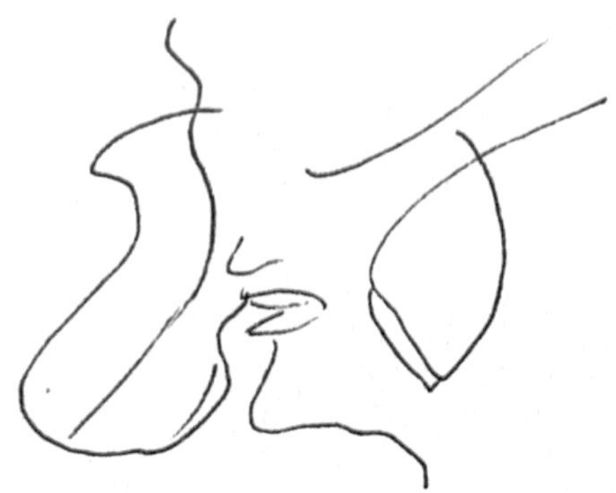

Breeze shaking my louvres
August came breaking in
whispering your name
and asked me to say goodbye
to the months that passed
to the pain I had
and to the love I lost

Silence prevailed
as I played my piano
I could feel your fingers,
underneath mine
there was life in me
in you
in our muted karaoke

(with you am alive)

Dance with me Romeo
our bottled dreams can wait

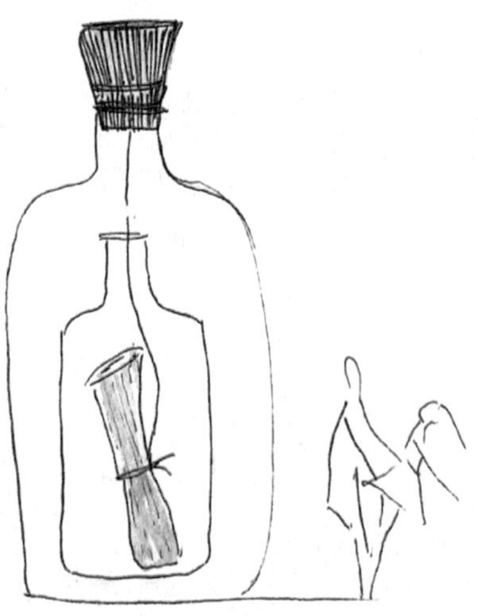

Every night, every eclipse
I watch you sleep
or was that a dejavu
that kept me awake?

I slept on your spell
as you watched me
from miles away
knowing that you're dreaming with me

And in that dream
I remember asking you to paint me
a high tide on a blue moon
as your horizon slid over mine

Stalking you
as you paint
colours to my sunset

(come back to bed)

The taste of cigars
on my painted lips
the torn ruffles of my elegant white
I see us in the moonlight
embracing the lustre,
writing lyrics
to our shared history
enveloping the breach
a memoire,
a picture,
living inside me
just like the dancing autumn leaves

The lights, the chaos
the silence, the break
this evening my love
you are my sunset

I barely look into the mirror
although I seek for that mere second
ticking inside me
telling me to hold on

I looked again
besides the blurred image
and the mumbling voices
but she had another story to tell
the one in which
'our time was never'

My tendrils tip-toed
to grab the cupid's bow

You are the amber to my April
and the twilight to my vineyard
you are the rhythm to my tides
and the Mozart to my notes
you are the legacy left behind
and the bee to my carpel
you are the poetry on my lips
and the blossom on my bed
fall back to my arms
I promise to be better this time
and with a thimble
I will close that chapter
of misery and war
subdue me as I mend our souls

Feel the fabric
between our ribs
as lust sew em
into one whole

Crush my armour
allow me to melt it,
for am your smith now
and you're my gold

I remember
the first time we held hands
'a chapter' from my velvet wishes
'a picture' framed on my wall

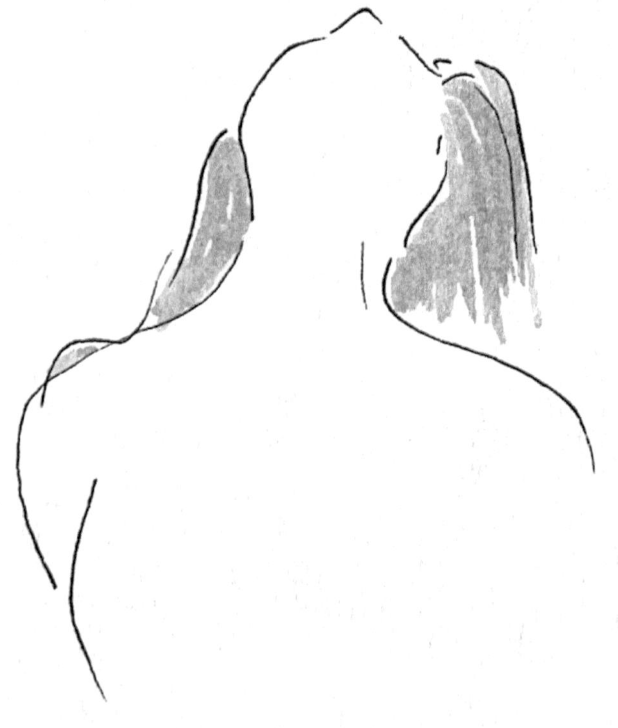

On a summer night
you, me
and the silence of the
pearls; sparkling on my spine

Remember?
how your fingers drew the map
to the treasure I saved
only for you to find

You opened me
on that melting moon
and wrote that song
as I composed

I was yours
to read, to write
like the beautiful grammar
in my rhyme

Early summer wind
sieging our favourite walks
remnants of Bleu de Chanel in air
your neck
mastering courage
yet vulnerable to my breath

(intimate than ever)

Arrows clearing out the coastal clouds
making the sky picture perfect
for the two of us
the frame I kept in my wounded chest;
felt like watching a vintage movie
with my eyes closed

(I will always love you)

Your eyes narrating
a thousand year old story
couldn't resist but stare
deep; I lost track of time
mist or magic
help me define this moment
for am about to surrender
before my strange addiction

(ours was different)

Perfect reflection of stars
gasping every silence
every picture
of you
of us
of our little benign love

(I remember)

Steer clear off our Champagne love
for let us not wake the muted colours
quiescent for years
I must say, I lost count

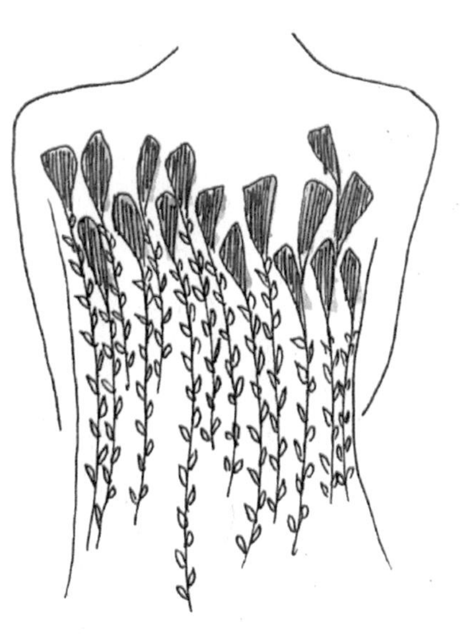

Embers of moonlight
watching us from above
sharing our little secrets
and that's when I wrote
my very first song

My sky and your blue
promises be flailing about
as the sterling in my eyes
kissed the setting sun

I'll let you guard the walls
to my rustic heart
and invite you in
just like old times

But promise me
you won't leave me broke
maybe my regrets
would tie us both

(I wish I knew)

I've been waiting
for the sea green waves
to take me deep;
deep beyond our
drugged dreams

(lost)

All hallows eve ignited our love
when we went together for ‘trick or treat’
down the lane
shouting happy halloween

(mere memories)

Craving for that mere touch
to feel the friction
again and again
thereby unfolding the magic within
oh my
am in one of your phantoms
aren't I?

I'd send a raven
on every blue moon
don't write me back
rather seed your essence
in the eastern cold winds

Writing you a song
felt like prison break
for you're my tranquillity;
my sin my saint

(my March is melting)

I fell in love
maybe that wasn't a choice
I made
for a second I thought
'I found my stolen scotch again'

Grey sky
you and me
yellow sweater
and our whiskey ways

(wake me up from this dream)

He opened me like a letter
as we took a walk
along the desperate violet vines
smiling in the sun

(my first)

Forgotten tales and champagne gold
her amber eyes
I'm in love I know

Day and night
past the secrets
past the neon sighs
I see us
and the art in your eyes

(we weren't broken)

Break my walls
feel me
my warmth
burn me -
alive in your kerosene kisses
for what its worth
I wanna be touched
by your magic hands

(until next time)

I'd be lying if I say
I didn't dream
of the busy road,
my August love
and your brimming moon

To grow old
with beautiful sags
here and there
wrinkled and frail

To hold hands
at the crossroads
partly blind
with clouds in our eyes

To watch the fireflies
gleam through the ashes
as we pour our last wine

AND THE ECLIPSE

Creamy clouds
brimming off
my coffee cup
slow and tense

Beethoven's moonlight
playing soft in my ears

Gazing at the polaroids
longer than I could remember

Receding footsteps;
fading vignette

Felt like a vintage dream
where I'm the paper doll
colouring my silhouettes
in peach and magic mint

And we became the known strangers
wanting to let go
and yet holding onto the fire
burning our suns

(after the eclipse)

I carried you
reminding myself
of all the pain and pleasure
I went through

I carried you
yet again
like a forgotten firewood
burning every splinters
resting in peace

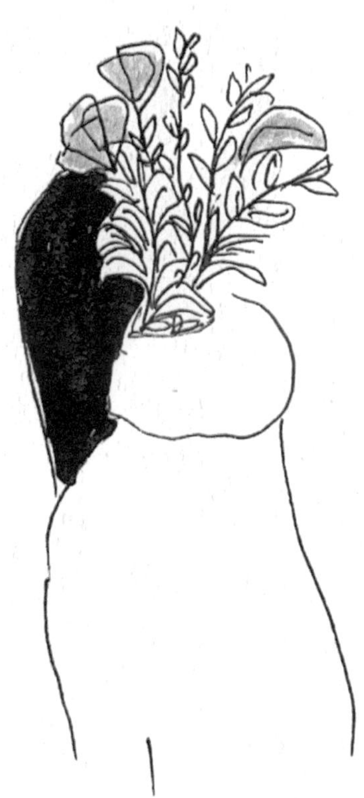

A hundred million years
and nothing changed
some violets did lie
amidst the chaos and pain

(bound by love)

The promises I never meant to keep
left my door open;
vulnerable
like the shattered crystal -
I ought not to break

My tears don't rush
nor do they pick the
Emeralds from the floor
at least not anymore

It was just me
and my secrets
taking a walk to wander

Doodle me
my entire world
for am the 'fleur'
withering lullabies
on your paper rings

My whereabouts; a standstill
my poetry flailing in my book
ripping my thoughts
unhinged
breathing blue air
holding it until my lungs wailed
your name
hear me for once
am in pain

Save me from me
before I lose my sanity

Me and my broken compass
seeking for answers
unanswered
out in the dark woods
where our folklore
howled in vain

(our eclipse)

Searching for the voices
that once left me shattered

(tyranny of the empty room)

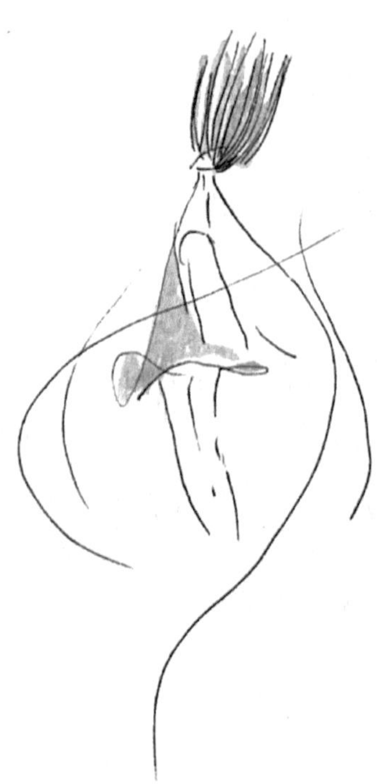

After all
this misbegotten Mardi Gras wedding
is nothing more than a charade
a poignant reminder
‘my morbid day’

(the wedding)

And then there's
the fraction of seconds
and am zoning out; I hear
silence amidst the chaos
the happiest version of myself
I guess I was never lost
after all

(breathe)

Incomplete and delusional
the gift of silence
liberating gravity
from the empty room
pain and endeavour
leaving beautiful scars
I'm healing as my stories
sew back my wings;
the stories that I keep to myself
the stories that rather be untold

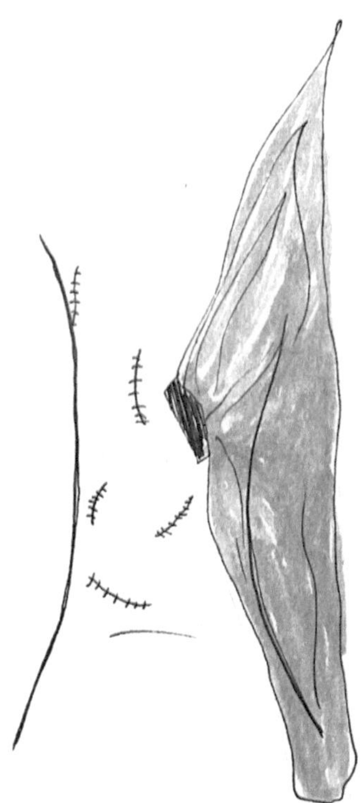

I'm the first born
spinning the Ferris wheel
for you
another merry round

The adrenaline rush
deluge of thoughts
wanting to escape
to run
far
far away

(Illusion)

I feel avenged
pure tranquility
and slowly the shadow of my shadow
segregated into infinite
spheres of serenity

(avenged)

I found my long lost surfboard
resting on the wall
built by my memories alone

(where am I?)

A part of me always wished
for you to turn back
and now that your heart is spoken for
perhaps I should find
peace in the abyss

Blinding lights
crushed inside my pocket
trying to break free
from the path that I did not chose,
from the fate am destined to be

(merely existing)

And all I have is this hallucinating faith in me
'that life would drop the veil
to my fantasies'

Oh thee
as I weep
being forgotten is yet another chapter
for you to read

Au revoir
my feet stone cold
am twice eleven
and my violin sore

I was a loyal puppet
dancing to your dramatic theme
despite the lustful lies
you painted on me

(regrets)

He found me shattered
and arranged me like a puzzle
although I wonder
why he stole that one missing piece

"Tell me about my day"
her voice crippled in fear

Tranquil music scarring
the ice inside your soul
to thaw the frozen rhyme
a love that consumed me
a lie that we vowed

I was too busy loving you
and hardly ever noticed
that you were planting
fake plastic trees
all these time

You let your ego grew wild
and it made you see me as a seer

Striking off every line
turning over to a new page
hoping this time
I won't picture you

To them
I'm the lonely loon
sitting idle by the sidewalk

To me
I'm the lifeless clown
painting scenic funfair on my canvas

The bonnets nearly kissed
and the veil just dropped back in
breaking the eerie silence
of the trauma -
I hid fathoms deep

Reinforce me and my hull
for you could never
cull my fugitive
my fugitive on the run!

The long lost memories
wanting to fade
benighted by me
drenched in fibs and fables
reaching out all night
the demons;
wanting a fair fight
and here I drown
like a weed
seeking for the
dandelions of the sea

I found happiness
it was right here with me
waiting to transcend

(drowning paper boat)

"Every floret of lavender heather
craved for her love, her touch"
the history you'll hear
from my paper boat
floating passive
down the living brook

Dear diary,
mind the paper mites
and those fraying pages
keep my cursives as secrets
like the naked walls in my boudoir
and open the blank page
that I left out to write
as I bleed melody
through my almond brown eyes

The city got me zoning
like a roadkill, I laid there
shredded
wondering about my stolen sunlight
until your gentle bristles -
stroked thin lines
of crimson and blue
over my cloudless sky

A chapter from our book
soaked in alchemy
a memory, evermore
for you
and for me

I tried to open the walls
to unhinge the promise of something new
I searched for the right word
as the enchanted lines
framed me a key
I held the key
gentle in my palms
for I cannot spare
the art that define hope

Sweet numbness slipping away
breaking the enchanted blue
engraved
quivering hands;
perhaps bound by the starlings
who lied about the tears that
shall drown the wind

I remember the huge waves
striding towards my castle
and the violets blooming
against their will
I remember the errors of the moon
being carved on the wall
for I shall fare you well
another beautiful milestone

Midnight blues
composing the breeze
as I took a walk

In every step
I was breathing art
soaked in slivers of joy

Strange yet beautiful
was the sound of my footsteps
each painting over
the emotions I left behind
by setting the scented memories free
from my hope
from my gravity

(a walk to remember)

Heather…

A picture that I kept to myself,

A story that I'd rather tell

ABOUT THE AUTHOR

Jasna Usman is a poet, an architect, a public speaker and an environmentalist. She started writing at the age of seven with her little scribblings in her journals. All of her writings were sealed inside her journals, until she decided to unveil 'Heather'. Her father moulded her poetic spirit and handed her all the support. At the age of 21, she got featured in online poetry communities, and won a Global poetry competition. She started writing this immersive collection of poetry while doing her third year in architecture. Besides narrating the story of a 23 year old woman, 'Heather' takes the reader's mind through the hardships; from 'questioning the very existence to finding her path to life'.

www.ingramcontent.com/pod-product-compliance
Ingram Content Group UK Ltd.
Pitfield, Milton Keynes, MK11 3LW, UK
UKHW040604210726
13854UKWH00009B/2619

9 789357 011884